C000082407

CREATIVE RECIPES FOR

# _H_ERBS

a Salamander book
**Published by Salamander Books Limited**
**LONDON • NEW YORK**

Published by Salamander Books Ltd.,
129-137 York Way, London N7 9LG, United Kingdom.

© Salamander Books Ltd., 1991

**ISBN 0 86101 601 7**

Distributed by Hodder and Stoughton Services, PO Box 6,
Mill Road, Dunton Green, Sevenoaks, Kent TN13 2XX.

## CREDITS

RECIPES BY: *Judy Bastyra, Mary Cadogan, Julia Canning,
Caroline Cowen, Carole Handslip, Kerenza Harries, Dolly Meers,
Janice Murfitt, Cecilia Norman, Lorna Rhodes, Sally Taylor,
Carol Timperley and Mary Trewby*

PHOTOGRAPHY BY: *David Gill, Paul Grater, David Johnson,
Alan Newnham, Jon Stewart and Graham Tann*

DESIGN BY: *Tim Scott*

TYPESET BY: *The Old Mill*

COLOUR SEPARATION BY: *P&W Graphics, Pte. Ltd.*

PRINTED IN BELGIUM BY: *Proost International Book Production,
Turnhout, Belgium*

# $\mathcal{C}$ONTENTS

# WATERCRESS SOUP WITH MARIGOLDS

*125 g (4 oz/⅔ cup) chick-peas*
*pinch of bicarbonate of soda*
*3 sprigs of thyme*
*6 teaspoons olive oil*
*1 leek, finely chopped*
*2 courgettes (zucchini), cubed*
*1 carrot, sliced*
*6 teaspoons finely chopped parsley*
*1.25 litres (36 fl oz/4½ cups) chicken stock*
*125 g (4 oz) watercress, finely chopped*
*3 marigold flowers, to garnish*

*P*ut chick-peas in a bowl, cover with cold water and soak for 2 hours. Put into a large saucepan with their soaking liquid, bicarbonate of soda and thyme; add water to cover chick-peas by about 10 cm (4 in). Bring to boil and boil steadily for 10 minutes. Lower heat, cover pan and simmer for 30-40 minutes or until soft. Drain chick-peas and discard thyme. In another saucepan, heat the oil. Add leek, courgettes (zucchini), carrot, parsley and chick-peas; cover and cook over gentle heat for 10 minutes, to soften vegetables. Pour on chicken stock and simmer for 15-20 minutes until tender. Add watercress. Purée soup in a blender or food processor until smooth. Serve immediately, garnished with marigold petals. *Serves 6*

# GOATS' CHEESE WITH MINT

*185 g (6 oz) goats' cheese*
*75 ml (2½ fl oz/⅓ cup) milk*
*3 teaspoons olive oil*
*1 teaspoon lemon juice*
*½ red pepper, seeded*
*4 teaspoons chopped mint*
*salt and pepper, to taste*
*sprigs of mint, to garnish*

*P*ress goats' cheese through a nylon sieve into a mixing bowl. Add milk, oil and lemon juice and blend well until mixture is smooth and creamy. Cut red pepper into thin strips, 5 cm (2 in) long. Fold into cheese mixture with chopped mint; season with salt and pepper.

Mould the cheese mixture into a flat round, about 15 cm (6 in) in diameter. Place on a serving plate, cover with plastic wrap and chill for at least 4 hours, to allow flavours to mingle.

Uncover the cheese and surround with sprigs of mint. Serve with crackers and biscuits. *Serves 4*

NOTE: A delicious starter which may alternatively be served at the end of the meal in place of cheese.

# SMOKED SALMON PARCELS

250 g (8 oz) smoked salmon
185 g (6 oz) cream cheese
6 teaspoons olive oil
2 teaspoons lime juice
9 teaspoons finely chopped dill weed
black pepper, to taste
4 teaspoons horseradish cream
lime slices and sprigs of dill, to garnish

*S*lightly oil four 100 ml (3½ fl oz / ⅓ cup) ramekin dishes. Line each with smoked salmon, moulding it to fit dish and leaving a little extra to fold over top of dish.

Blend cream cheese with oil and lime juice. Add chopped dill, black pepper and any extra smoked salmon, chopped. Spoon in horseradish but do not mix in thoroughly; it should be distributed in hot ribbons throughout cream cheese mixture.

Place 4-5 teaspoons cream cheese mixture in each ramekin, then fold smoked salmon over top to make a neat parcel. Chill for 3-4 hours.

To serve, turn out onto a plate. Garnish with lime slices and dill. *Serves 4*

# $\mathcal{H}$ERB BAKED EGGS

*4 thin slices ham*
*3 large eggs*
*1 teaspoon prepared mustard*
*60 ml (2 fl oz/¼ cup) Greek yogurt*
*90 g (3 oz) mature Cheddar cheese, finely grated*
*2 teaspoons chopped fresh chives*
*2 teaspoons chopped fresh parsley*
*fresh herbs, to garnish*
*slices of hot buttered toast, to serve*

Preheat the oven to 180C (350F/Gas 4). Line 4 greased ramekins with ham slices. Beat together eggs, mustard and Greek yogurt.

Stir 60 g (2 oz/¼ cup) of the cheese into the egg mixture. Mix together chives and parsley and add half to the mixture. Stir well, then spoon into prepared ramekins. Sprinkle with remaining cheese and herbs and bake in the oven for 25-30 minutes until golden and set.

Serve in the ramekins, garnished with fresh herbs. Serve the baked eggs with slices of hot buttered toast. *Serves 4*

# CHAMPAGNE OYSTERS

*48 oysters, cleaned*
*125 g (4 oz) butter*
*2 tablespoons finely chopped spring onion*
*2 teaspoons chopped tarragon*
*1 teaspoon chopped mint*
*375 ml (12 fl oz/1½ cups) champagne*
*salt and pepper, to taste*
*sprigs of mint, to garnish*

To open oysters, hold with absorbent kitchen paper on a work surface, flatter shell uppermost and hinged end towards you. Insert the point of an oyster knife into the gap in the hinge and twist the blade to snap shells apart. Slide blade along the inside of the upper shell to sever the muscle. Discard empty half shells. Remove any broken shell from the oyster with the point of the knife. Remove oysters from shells and set aside. Arrange shells in a circle on 4 individual serving plates.

In a saucepan, melt 30 g (1 oz) butter, add spring onion, tarragon and mint and cook for 1 minute. Add champagne and salt and pepper, bring to the boil, then simmer until liquid is reduced by half. Whisk in remaining butter a piece at a time, until sauce is thickened and creamy. Add oysters to sauce and cook gently for 2 minutes. Spoon oysters back into shells, covering each with a little sauce. Garnish with mint. *Serves 4*

# NEW ENGLAND CLAM CHOWDER

*two 315 g (10 oz) cans clams*
*90 g (3 oz) back bacon, rinded and diced*
*1 onion, finely chopped*
*500 g (1 lb) potatoes, diced*
*315 ml (10 fl oz/1¼ cups) fish stock*
*315 ml (10 fl oz/1¼ cups) milk*
*155 ml (5 fl oz/⅔ cup) single (light) cream*
*pinch dried thyme*
*salt and pepper*
*fresh thyme leaves or paprika, to garnish*

*D*rain clams, reserving liquid, then chop and set aside. Put bacon into a saucepan and fry over high heat until fat runs and bacon is lightly browned. Add onion and cook until soft, then add potatoes, liquid from clams, fish stock and milk. Bring to the boil, then cover and simmer for about 20 minutes, or until potatoes are tender.

Stir in cream, clams, thyme and salt and pepper, then reheat for a few minutes: do not boil. Serve garnished with thyme or paprika. *Serves 6*

# *L*AMB WITH MUSTARD AND TARRAGON

1 boned shoulder of lamb, about 2 kg (4 lb)
2 cloves garlic, slivered
4 teaspoons dry mustard
2 teaspoons salt
3-4 sprigs of tarragon
black pepper, to taste
3 teaspoons olive oil
30 g (1 oz) butter
1 onion, finely sliced
200 ml (6½ fl oz/¾ cup) white wine
3 teaspoons chopped tarragon

*P*reheat oven to 180C (350F/Gas 4). Make several slits in lamb and insert garlic. Mix together mustard and salt and smear half on inside of the lamb. Lay tarragon sprigs on meat and grind some black pepper over. Roll up and secure with string. Rub outside of joint with remaining mustard and salt. In a flameproof dish, heat oil and butter, add lamb and brown. Add onion and soften, then pour in wine; stir and scrape up all juices and sediment. Cover and cook in the oven for 2½-3 hours, to taste. Allow lamb to stand for 10 minutes before serving. Pour fat off cooking juices, then simmer for several minutes, stirring. Remove string from meat and carve; add chopped tarragon to sauce. *Serves 6-8*

# $\mathscr{H}$ICKORY SMOKED
## CHICKEN

*2 handfuls hickory smoking chips*
*a handful of mixed fresh herbs*
*1.5-2 kg (3-4 lb) oven-ready chicken*
*salt*

*C*ook this dish in a kettle barbecue or wet smoker. Soak hickory chips in hot water. Light barbecue and when coals are hot, sprinkle with well-drained hickory chips.

Put herbs in a shallow metal dish of hot water. Place on rack over coals. Season surface of chicken with salt to taste and place on a metal rack over water pan. Close barbecue lid.

Reduce heat and cook chicken over low coals for about 3 hours, turning every 30 minutes. The pan of hot water may need topping up during cooking. To do this, move chicken to one side and add water with extreme caution. The cooked chicken will be moist with faintly pink-tinged flesh and a distinctive smoky flavour. *Serves 4-6*

# $\mathcal{P}$ORK WITH HERBS

1 pork tenderloin, about 500 g (1 lb), well trimmed
4 teaspoons plain flour
4 teaspoons single (light) cream
oregano sprigs and sage leaves, to garnish
6 teaspoons olive oil
3 teaspoons Madeira
½ teaspoon salt
½ teaspoon black pepper
1 teaspoon Dijon wholegrain mustard
1 teaspoon caster sugar
3 teaspoons grated onion
3 teaspoons chopped fresh sage, to garnish
3 teaspoons chopped fresh oregano, to garnish

To make marinade, blend oil, Madeira, salt, pepper, mustard, sugar, onion, sage and oregano together. Pour over pork tenderloin in a shallow ovenproof bowl and turn to coat evenly. Cover and cool for 2-3 hours. Preheat oven to 220C (425F/Gas 7). Cook pork for 15 minutes, until tender and cooked through. Keep warm. Stir flour into remaining marinade in dish and pour into a saucepan. Bring to the boil and cook for 2 minutes. Remove from heat and stir in cream. Slice the pork into 1 cm (½ in) slices and pour sauce on to a serving plate. Arrange sliced pork on top and garnish. *Serves 4*

# $S$MOKED FISH PLATTER

2 smoked trout fillets
2 peppered smoked mackerel fillets
3 slices bread, toasted
30 g (1 oz/6 teaspoons) butter
1 teaspoon lemon juice
100 g (3½ oz) can smoked oysters, drained
small lettuce leaves, lemon slices and parsley or dill, to garnish
HORSERADISH SAUCE:
3 tablespoons Greek strained yogurt
2 teaspoons horseradish relish
1 teaspoon lemon juice
2 teaspoons chopped fresh parsley
pepper

*S*kin trout and mackerel fillets and carefully cut them into small even-sized pieces. Set them aside.

Using a small fancy cutter, cut out 4 rounds from each toast. Beat butter and lemon juice together. Spread a little on the toast rounds. Place a smoked oyster on each buttered toast round.

Arrange the pieces of smoked fish and the oysters on toast on 4 plates. Garnish each plate with a few lettuce leaves, lemon slices and parsley or dill.

Make sauce by mixing ingredients together in a bowl. Spoon into a serving dish and serve with salads. *Serves 4*

# TAMARILLO & PASTA SALAD

500 g (1 lb) dried pasta shells
90 ml (3 fl oz / ⅓ cup) olive oil
3 tamarillos, peeled and sliced thinly
185 g (6 oz) goat's cheese, sliced or crumbled
125 ml (4 fl oz / ½ cup) olive oil
90 ml (3 fl oz / ⅓ cup) red wine vinegar
2 cloves garlic, crushed
1 green pepper, seeded and chopped
1 small onion, chopped
125 g (4 oz) canned pimento, drained
3 tablespoons chopped parsley
3 tablespoons chopped basil
salt and pepper, to taste
sprigs of basil, to garnish

*I*n a large saucepan, cook pasta in boiling salted water for 8-10 minutes or until just cooked (*al dente*). Drain, rinse under tepid water and drain thoroughly. Transfer to a large bowl and evenly coat with olive oil. Cover with plastic wrap and chill for 30 minutes. To make dressing: put all ingredients in a blender or food processor and work until smooth. Pour dressing over pasta and toss well. Add tamarillos and goat's cheese to pasta and toss very gently. Transfer to individual serving plates and garnish with basil. Serve immediately. *Serves 6*

# $\mathcal{F}$ESTIVE DIP SELECTION

1 small aubergine (eggplant)
2 cloves garlic
125 ml (4 fl oz/½ cup) thick sour cream
salt and ground black pepper
3 teaspoons chopped fresh rosemary
250 g (8 oz/1 cup) cream cheese
6 teaspoons fromage frais
30 g (1 oz/¼ cup) chopped fresh mixed herbs
125 g (4 oz/⅔ cup) red lentils, cooked in 470 ml
(15 fl oz/1¾ cups) water
155 ml (5 fl oz/⅔ cup) Greek yogurt
mixed vegetable sticks

*P*reheat oven to 220C (425F/Gas 7). Bake aubergine (eggplant) until skin has charred and flesh is tender, turning once. Cut aubergine (eggplant) in half, scoop out flesh; cool. Using a food processor, add aubergine (eggplant), 1 clove garlic, thick sour cream, salt and pepper to taste and rosemary; process until smooth and creamy. Place cream cheese, fromage frais, mixed herbs and salt and pepper in a bowl and beat until soft and well blended. Process remaining garlic, salt and pepper to taste, lentils and yogurt until creamy and smooth. Serve dips in small bowls accompanied by mixed vegetable sticks. *Each dip serves 6-8*

# $C$HICKEN & GRAPE SALAD

*500 g (1 lb) cooked cold chicken, cut into small dice*
*3 sticks celery, chopped*
*125 g (4 oz) black grapes*
*125 g (4 oz) green grapes*
*½ lettuce, finely shredded, if desired*
*nasturtium flowers and tarragon sprigs, to garnish*
*TARRAGON CREAM DRESSING:*
*3 tablespoons virgin olive oil*
*1 tablespoon tarragon vinegar*
*3 tablespoons thick sour cream*
*salt and pepper*

*P*ut chicken and celery in a bowl. Halve grapes, remove pips and add to the bowl.

To make the dressing, mix all the ingredients together in a bowl or screw-top jar. Pour over salad and toss together. Divide lettuce, if using, between 4 plates and spoon chicken salad on top. Serve garnished with nasturtium flowers and tarragon.

*Serves 4 as a main course*

# Asparagus
## WITH CHICORY

*250 g (8 oz) asparagus spears, trimmed*
*3 heads of chicory*
*250 g (8 oz/1 cup) cream cheese*
*3 slices of Parma ham*
*1 tangerine*
*½ clove garlic, crushed*
*¼ teaspoon salt and ground black pepper*
*½ teaspoon Dijon mustard*
*2 teaspoons clear honey*
*4 teaspoons olive oil*
*2 teaspoons chopped fresh tarragon*

*H*alf-fill a shallow flameproof dish with water and bring to the boil. Add asparagus and cook for 3-4 minutes until tender, then drain and cool. To make marinade, cut tangerine peel finely, squeeze juice from fruit and place in a bowl with garlic, salt, pepper, mustard, honey, oil and tarragon. Beat until thoroughly blended. Pour over asparagus; cover and chill for at least 1 hour. Separate chicory leaves and cut into 2.5 cm (1 in) lengths. Spread a little cream cheese onto each leaf. Cut asparagus spears into 2.5 cm (1 in) lengths and place a length onto each chicory leaf. Cut ham into thin strips and wrap a piece around each chicory leaf. Garnish with strips of tangerine peel, reserved from marinade. *Makes 48*

# $O$ATMEAL CHIVE PANCAKES

60 g (2 oz/½ cup) plain flour
30 g (1 oz/¼ cup) fine oatmeal
pinch salt
2 large eggs
315 ml (10 fl oz/1¼ cups) milk
1 tablespoon chopped fresh chives
vegetable oil
8 thin slices smoked ham
30 g (1 oz/6 teaspoons) butter
4 large eggs, beaten
1 tablespoon chopped fresh chives
1-2 tablespoons single (light) cream
salt and pepper
fresh herbs, to garnish

*S*ift flour, oatmeal and salt into a large bowl, add the 2 eggs, milk and chives and beat until smooth. Heat and oil a 15 cm (6 in) pancake pan. Cover the base of the pan with batter and cook for 2 minutes. Turn the pancake over and top with a slice of ham whilst underside is cooking. Remove from pan and keep warm. Melt butter in a small pan, pour in the beaten eggs and cook over a low heat, stirring until thickened. Remove from the heat and stir in the chives and cream and season. Add filling to pancake and roll up. Garnish and serve immediately. *Serves 8*

# HALOUMI & MINT BREAD

*15 g (½ oz/3 teaspoons) fresh yeast*
*315 ml (10 fl oz/1¼ cups) warm water*
*250 g (8 oz/1¾ cups) wholewheat flour*
*250 g (8 oz/2 cups) plain flour*
*1 teaspoon salt*
*1 tablespoon olive oil*
*175g (6 oz) haloumi cheese, diced*
*3 tablespoons chopped mint*
*1 tablespoon sesame seeds*

$C$ream yeast with a little of the water; leave until frothy. Put flours and salt in a bowl; make a well in the centre. Add yeast mixture, remaining water and oil and mix to a soft dough.

Knead on a lightly floured surface for about 5 minutes, until smooth and elastic. Put into a clean bowl, cover and leave to rise in a warm place for 1½-2 hours. Preheat oven to 230C (450F/Gas 8). Turn dough onto a floured surface and punch into a flattish round. Fold in cheese and mint and knead for about 5 minutes. Shape into a circle and press out into a 20.5 cm (8 in) round. Put on a floured baking sheet and make a cut 2.5 cm (1 in) from the edge, right through to the bottom, all the way round. Brush with water and sprinkle with sesame seeds. Bake in the oven for 10 minutes; lower temperature to 200C (400F/Gas 6) and bake for 20 minutes. Cool on a wire rack. *Makes 1 loaf*

# ALMOND BLANCMANGE

*90 g (3 oz/½ cup) whole blanched almonds*
*4 egg yolks*
*125 g (4 oz/½ cup) caster sugar*
*375 ml (12 fl oz/1½ cups milk)*
*3 teaspoons powdered gelatine*
*250 ml (8 fl oz/1 cup) whipping cream*
*toasted flaked almonds and herb sprigs, to decorate*

*T*oast whole blanched almonds, turning frequently to brown evenly. Cool and grind coarsely in a coffee grinder or food processor. In a bowl, beat egg yolks and sugar until thick and mousse-like. Put milk into a saucepan and bring almost to boiling point. Beat into egg mixture. Return to saucepan, and stir over low heat until mixture has thickened sufficiently to coat the back of the spoon. Do not boil. Remove from heat and leave to cool. Sprinkle gelatine over 3 tablespoons water in a small bowl and leave to soften for 2-3 minutes. Stand bowl in a saucepan of hot water and stir until gelatine has dissolved. Stir into the milk mixture.

In another bowl, whip cream lightly. When milk mixture is on point of setting, stir in ground almonds and fold in cream. Spoon into a serving dish and chill until set. When ready to serve, decorate with toasted flaked almonds and herb sprigs. *Serves 6*

# GRAPEFRUIT & MINT SORBET

*185 g (6 oz/¾ cup) caster sugar*
*125 ml (4 fl oz/½ cup) water*
*juice of 2 grapefruit*
*juice of 1 lime*
*1 tablespoon finely chopped mint leaves*
*2 egg whites*
*3 kiwi fruit*
*sprigs of mint, to decorate*

*I*n a saucepan, heat sugar and water gently until sugar is dissolved, then boil steadily for 5 minutes; leave to cool. Strain grapefruit and lime juices into a bowl. Stir in the cooled syrup and chopped mint. Turn into a freezerproof container, cover and freeze for 2-3 hours, until half-frozen.

Whisk egg whites until stiff, then fold into half-frozen mixture. Return to freezer until just firm, then beat thoroughly and freeze until required.

Peel the kiwi fruit and purée them in a blender or food processor; sieve to remove pips.

To serve, cover plates with kiwi purée. Using 2 dessert spoons, shape ovals of sorbet and arrange three on each plate. Decorate with mint leaves and serve immediately. *Serves 4*

# TART LEMON MOULD

*625 ml (20 fl oz/2½ cups) milk*
*90 g (3 oz/⅓ cup) granulated sugar*
*3 teaspoons powdered gelatine*
*3 small egg yolks*
*grated peel and juice of 1 large lemon*
*90 g (3 oz/⅓ cup) caster sugar*
*lemon twists and herb sprigs, to decorate*

*P*ut milk, granulated sugar and gelatine into a small saucepan and set over a low heat. Bring almost to boiling point (but do not boil), stirring constantly. Remove from heat.

In a bowl, beat egg yolks together lightly and gradually pour hot milk over them, stirring all the time. Pour into a 940 ml (30 fl oz/3¾ cup) mould. Leave at room temperature until cold, then refrigerate until set.

While mixture is cooling, put grated lemon peel and juice into a small saucepan with caster sugar and stir over a low heat until sugar has dissolved. Leave to cool. When ready to serve, turn out pudding onto a serving plate and pour lemon syrup around it. Decorate with lemon twists and herbs. *Serves 4*